Celtic Nature Designs

COLORING BOOK

CARI BUZIAK

DOVER PUBLICATIONS
GARDEN CITY, NEW YORK

Thirty-one intricate images combine Celtic symbolism with beautiful nature motifs. Traditional knot designs and crosses are complemented by gorgeous birds, butterflies, fish, flowers, leaves, seashells, and other decorative natural ornaments. The illustrations are printed on one side only, and the pages are perforated for easy removal and display.

Bibliographical Note

Celtic Nature Designs Coloring Book, first published by Dover Publications in 2022, is a republication of thirty-one illustrations from *Celtic Nature Coloring Book*, published by Dover Publications in 2016.

International Standard Book Number
ISBN-13: 978-0-486-85019-1
ISBN-10: 0-486-85019-6

Manufactured in the United States of America
85019601   2022
www.doverpublications.com